Terms and Conditions

LEGAL NOTICE

The Publisher has strived to be as accurate and complete as possible in the creation of this report, notwithstanding the fact that he does not warrant or represent at any time that the contents within are accurate due to the rapidly changing nature of the Internet.

While all attempts have been made to verify information provided in this publication, the Publisher assumes no responsibility for errors, omissions, or contrary interpretation of the subject matter herein. Any perceived slights of specific persons, peoples, or organizations are unintentional.

In practical advice books, like anything else in life, there are no guarantees of income made. Readers are cautioned to reply on their own judgment about their individual circumstances to act accordingly.

This book is not intended for use as a source of legal, business, accounting or financial advice. All readers are advised to seek services of competent professionals in legal, business, accounting and finance fields.

You are encouraged to print this book for easy reading.

Table Of Contents

Forward

Chapter 1: About The Business

Chapter 2: About Leaders

Chapter 3: Marketing Systems

Chapter 4: Business Models

Chapter 5: Being A Success On The Net

Chapter 6: What You Need To Profit

Chapter 7: Integrity

Wrapping Up

Foreword

Success is accomplished by being willing to resist the odds, take the 'road less traveled,' and recognizing that the dandiest power you have, is already inside you.

In my own travel to success, I've discovered that the majority of what is offered online is really misleading and full of empty hopes. I came to discover success through partnering with the correct individuals and applying good old fashioned horse sense and smart business practices, to Network Marketing.

As a consequence, I've been able to walk off from my corporate job, travel the world with my life partner, all while establishing a net business that works for me.

My goal is to assist you in doing the same" that is, somebody who's ready to step away from the masses, and establish a true business that may bring you the personal and financial freedom you want.

Discovering The Underground Home Business Revolution Build The Right Attitude And Learn The Secrets Of Those Secretly Cashing In Big Time In The Comfort Of Their Homes.

Chapter 1:

About The Business

Synopsis

If you've been involved with the Net home business industry for any time at all, you likely realize there's a ton of junk online!

Everybody claims to have the "one" lead generation tactic that's going to help you blow away the rivalry, the "one wizardly pill" that's going to make all your Net marketing dreams come true.

At a particular level, individuals know that the Net is full of hype. It's like reading a magazine with an ad for a luxury auto and shows a fine-looking guy with the gorgeous girl. At a conscious level, individuals know it's an ad. But at a different level, individuals trust it.

Those sorts of ads are targeting something much richer than our conscious wants.

Great marketing targets people's core desires. An individual's want to be treasured, to feel worthy, to feel unparalleled and like s/he has a purpose.

The "make money" industry online operates in the same way. At a superficial level, most individuals understand the Net is full of hype. But there's this other part of the human mind, the emotional part, which would like to trust some part of it's true.

The Basics

So even though you recognize there's a ton of hype everyplace, it's really simple to get rolled up in all of it. And it adds up, as the Net is flooded with so many individuals. What's not to love? The dream to stay home in your jammies, work from anyplace with your laptop, and make buckets of revenue living like a rock-star... Correct?

There are individuals simply looking to make a half-time income, individuals who are looking to replace a full-time income, and those who are attempting to get rich fast. The excellent thing about the Net is that it levels the playing field in a lot of ways. But, simply because the Net levels the playing field, doesn't mean you automatically succeed.

A level field means that there's opportunity for everybody. However, it's a game. Understanding the game will be the difference between making it or simply wasting an immense amount of time and cash. The chilling truth is that for most individuals who come online... It's a tremendous cash cavity. Individuals trust that all they have to do is "follow the leader" and they're going to hit it rich. After all, that's what the site said—right? Right...

Individuals drop 1000s and 1000s of dollars for products that, ultimately, are not products anybody would purchase off the shelf. Basically, people are buying these products for the "right to sell and collect a profit'" on them. That's the bottom line, regardless how it's disguised.

Take a look at the immense number of business opportunities out there selling products. Many of the products are not anything that a consumer would purchase for that price off the shelf—or at any price for that matter. The mere reason why the products are selling is because marketers are purchasing them, to qualify to be in a place to sell them also. Apart from dropping 1000s of dollars for the products affiliated with a company, there's likewise the cost of all the training and tools.

It's simple to get caught in the cycle of buying every "hot" traffic-generating course that appears, big-ticket events, expensive PPC campaigns, more training courses, more monthly memberships, etcetera. Before you recognize it, you're out $50K and still have no clue what it takes to develop a successful online business.

This industry is full of exceedingly bright people who have had really successful careers. But it appears that somehow, when individuals come online, all "real world" horse sense exits. But disregarding your "gut" and your hunch comes with a really steep price—one that many individuals online are willing to pay to gratify their needs to trust in "an easy way to wealth".

It's the Net! Everything is quicker and cheaper, correct?

Now a Net Business is decidedly quicker and cheaper than most other business models, comparatively speaking. But this doesn't imply that simply signing on for a program and "following steps" are going to make you wealthy—as many of the opportunities out there say.

But having an Net business has a whole list of unbelievable advantages if you understand what you're doing and take the time to

set up your business like a true business and not something that you're simply going to "try out" to see if you bring in any cash.

Consider a franchise for instance. If you had to drop $300K for a little franchise and show up there each day to make it work and get it off the ground— chances are you wouldn't be thinking, "Well, let's simply see if this works. If it doesn't, I'll attempt something else." More than probably, you're going to throw it everything you've got for at least 2-4 years to make it work out. On the Net you may begin a business and make it profitable in much less time and with much less start-up capital than a traditional business or a franchise.

Before we go any farther, I wish to be clear on something. My goal in this e-Book is to educate you. I'm not the judge of what is correct and incorrect. My goal is to share with you the data that let me navigate my way through this hype-filled yet opportunity-filled industry, and to finally produce a sustainable and fruitful business.

Individuals will go to zealous efforts to ignore good sense and trust in the hype. Ignoring the voice of reality, your hunch and your gut has a steep price—a price a lot of individuals are willing to pay. That price is in the form of 1000s of dollars squandered and time spent— months or even years—chasing that one illusive wizardly traffic pill that, actually, doesn't exist. Sure, there are a few kick ass ways to drive enormous amounts of traffic, but it's not like switching on a light switch.

Success takes persistence in mastering a fresh skill set, being willing to put yourself out there and, most especially, listening to your hunch. But this is all easier said than done, particularly when the "leaders" that you believe you're supposed to be hearing have been occupying your head with fluff.

Even as you have to use care when getting involved with any business opportunity—selecting whom you seek advice and guidance from ought to be chosen with even as much care, if not more. It's well known that most individuals marketing a business online are swamped. It's difficult not to be. It's like learning an alien language. The simple way to learn an alien language is to absorb yourself in that culture and to be best buds with a native.

So the same idea applies to learning anything else new, including Net Marketing. It adds up that you not only get involved with the community, but that you network with and hear individuals who have been around the block.

Not only may being involved with a group of leaders cut your learning curve, but it may likewise supply a level of comfort that humans naturally look for. It's the same reason that faith is so mighty.

Regardless of what your particular religious and/or spiritual feelings are, among the basic reasons religion is so mighty is as it supplies answers to the unknown. The human mind is a bit funny when attempting to deal with the unknown. Many times, it merely can't. As a result, mankind gravitates towards anything that supplies answers and direction.

This is why alleged "leaders" exist in the Net Marketing arena. As they've answers and may supply direction.

But I do want to challenge you to take a hard look at who you follow and how come.

Chapter 2:

About Leaders

Synopsis

What Is True Leadership?

To me, Leadership isn't self-seeking. What does self-seeking imply?

Let's utilize a realistic illustration with our friend "Jim". Jim sells a business opportunity and says on all of his sites that he's a leader. Jim tells the individuals who follow him—those who join his business opportunity—that in order to be a leader, they ought to "give back". And that only the individuals who "give back" are thought leaders.

So of course, when Jim wants somebody to host a training call, produce training, make follow-up calls, or do anything else that's going to help Jims business, he's a ready group of "volunteers."

These volunteers are charged up at the prospect of stepping up to the plate and volunteering their time in exchange for the acknowledgement and status that comes with being one of Jims "leaders".

It appears to make sense. There are individuals in Jim's downline who require help and by providing this help; the volunteers are thought to be leaders. This is something that happens daily in many different organizations and downlines in this industry.

Looking At Leaders

As a result, there's a basic belief that by being a handmaid, you're being a leader. Actually, the "leaders" are merely followers who donate their time to another persons cause. The only leader in this situation is Jim.

This common misconception gets individuals—who even might be top producers—wedged in a web of trusting that by assisting, they're being leaders. And so as they spend all their time being in the limelight, demonstrating their leadership while their own real beliefs fall by the wayside and start to disintegrate and no more exist.

The true leader's notions become the volunteers' own notions. They forget who they are truly are, what they truly signify, and what is it they really want.

Their brand becomes one associated with assisting the "greater institution" (Jim's organization). And now the chances of these volunteers ("leaders") ever quitting their volunteer work is thin to none.

Jim knows this, so he's happy. As the volunteers' whole persona gets so engrained with Jims notions and wants—they believe Jim's beliefs and wants are their own. The volunteers will now champion Jims cause at any cost, whether or not this cause is morally bankrupt.

A true leader is somebody that's willing to risk his or her own fate, to do what they notion is correct. This implies going against the grain—taking a stand when there are 1000s of individuals who will gladly throw stones.

A true leader is in the end assisting an outside cause that he believes in, for the purpose of assisting that cause—not merely to earn followers. Sure, the leader will likely acquire followers as a result, but this isn't the only purpose of a true leader's charge.

A leader isn't concerned with whether or not he earns followers. His chief focus is in accomplishing the goals or cause that he believes in. The followers are merely an effect.

True leaders don't have time to be "volunteers" for Jim, or handmaids for those in need of "help". They're too busy fighting for what they trust in and working to accomplish their own goals affiliated with their own cause.

This implies that on the outside, being a "handmaid" of the industry or "Jims XYZ Marketing System" might appear to comprise leadership. But, it's the exact opposite.

While this is a really clever marketing technique utilized in a lot of different ways in the "make cash online" industry, you now have the knowledge to differentiate what a true leader is.

And by bearing this knowledge, you may start to question who you're following—and why. Ultimately, this will likewise push you to stand up for what YOU trust in.

This will push you to stick up for YOUR cause. Not your sponsor's cause or anybody else's, but your own.

Ultimately, you'll gain the most gratification and fulfillment out of life by remaining true to your instincts, regardless of what others believe.

It's a tragedy to see how willing individuals are to forget about what they trust in, and to adopt a "leader's" fresh beliefs for the hope of making a couple of thousands dollars.

My goal in discussing this matter is to challenge what occurs in this industry—in hopes that you never lose yourself and what you really believe in.

For as long as individuals continue to chase this, they'll be forever stuck in the unprofitable cycle of hype.

I encourage you to begin listening to your hunch and your gut. It's an excellent gift that you have for a reason. It's there to guide you and will provide you the cutting edge in an industry where the myth of cash frequently quiets any voice of reason.

But utilizing your hunch, horse sense, and treating your business like a business will bring you payoffs far greater than any empty promise.

My goal is to help you take charge over what you listen to and where your focus is—to produce a Net Business that is not only successful, but satisfying too.

Chapter 3:
Marketing Systems

Synopsis

"Everything you require to accomplish your dreams, in one place!"

Mmm...Sounds alluring, right?

I want to dive into one of the most popular platforms in the Net business industry today, and that's "Marketing Systems".

If you hear the term "Marketing System", you may question what the heck I'm discussing. So first, let's specify what I mean when utilizing the term "Marketing System".

The Platform

In this industry, here's what a Marketing System commonly looks like:

- You join the Marketing System for a monthly membership fee.
- After paying your monthly fee, you're now a member.
- You've access to a community of other Net entrepreneurs.
- You've access to training and other resources.
- The Marketing System probably provides a series of sites, or a "Sales Funnel" that you may utilize.
- The sites are commonly generic with maybe several customization choices.

Here's some of the appeal to join a Marketing System…

- You get to "connect" to a system that's "demonstrated" to work.
- Rather than attempting to work out how to grow your business online by yourself, you may leverage the experience of others.
- You acquire access to a whole community of individuals who are just like you, building a net business.
- You've leaders to follow who are going to tell you what to do.
- Everything is laid out in a "Step-By-Step" fashion.
- You don't have to try and "re-invent the wheel".
- You see others claiming they've made cash with the system. It appears really simple: You sign up, you follow the leader, you make cash.

So the question arises then, "If the Marketing System is so easy, than why isn't everybody doing it and why isn't everybody in the system making an absolute killing?"

And that's a great question that a lot of individuals ask, but few get a true answer to. If you've considered signing up in a business opportunity and asked this question from your likely sponsor, you likely received one of the following answers:

- Some individuals simply don't trust it's possible for them.
- Some individuals are simply too lazy and don't wish to make it work.
- Most individuals aren't willing to do the work.
- Some individuals are bad at following directions and attempt to reinvent the wheel.

Now, there's a lot of truth to these answers. In business...

- It's true that many individuals are limited by their own notions.
- It's true that some individuals are simply lazy and don't wish to make it work.
- Some individuals are bad at following directions and are perpetually attempting to reinvent the wheel.

However, there's a greater truth that most individuals give little attention to. And that's that the Marketing System, in and of itself, is a business. Meaning, the people who run the business are running a "for profit" business—not a gratis help center.

The truth that I wish to highlight is that the individuals who own the systems are not inevitably making cash doing the things or selling the products that they're telling YOU to do.

Let me repeat: Owning a Marketing System is a for profit business. As the owner, you make cash by collecting membership fees, affiliate commissions, and JV profits.

Yet most individuals are under the assumption that, in fact, the individuals featured as the main story inside the system are making all their cash doing the precise thing you're going to be doing. It appears logical from the surface, and that's commonly what is advertised to get you in the door.

But realize: it's virtually impossible for you to earn the type of cash that's claimed on a sustainable basis, by merely "following the leader".

Cash is made through mighty branding, enterprising marketing and above all else, understanding the business that you're in.
Making revenue with a Net business is about understanding the game that you've voluntarily decided to take part in.

The bulk of what's online is a game of changing perception to facilitate impulsive purchasing. Owning a Marketing System is likewise a game. A totally different game than being a member who's marketing something.

Comprehend that the incentive to keep you around and paying your monthly subscription is the top priority for the owners of the system.

As a result, you'll discover that a lot of systems have long drawn out processes that you supposedly need to go through with.

The more you have to learn and the more info you have to go through, the more subscription fees will be accumulated from you.

All of the "nuts and bolts" data inside the majority of marketing systems available may likely be put together in 50-page PDF,

summarizing everything inside the system. But the chances of that sort of business model making a substantial and sustainable profit for the owners are slender to none. Individuals would purchase the PDF and be on their way.

But, utilizing a continuity based business model (meaning that individuals are billed continually) along with adding all sorts of time-consuming fluff makes for a much better margin of profit.

Here's what I wish you to comprehend:
If you are a member of a Marketing System, you are a number. Most individuals are working for the system to grow it, rather than using the system to grow their own business.
There's a big difference here.

If the individuals who owned the system truly wished to teach you how to make revenue the same way they did, they'd teach you how to set up your own Marketing System. It's an easy as that.

After all, that's really how they're making their cash.

They don't teach you that for a rationality. The cost of setting up your own system takes an enormous amount of resources, time, sweat and experience.

So there's clearly a benefit to becoming a member. You don't have to get the cost and expertise to set up your own system. Owning a Marketing System, in and of itself, is a totally different business model than really marketing a business opportunity or products online.

Chapter 4:

Business Models

Synopsis

You and I both know the Net is full of many different ways to make cash. While the Net presents tremendous opportunity, it's become increasingly hard to keep track of the different business models.

After some time, all the opportunities start to look the same and it's difficult to tell what the true differences are.

Everybody claims that their way is "The Ultimate Money-Making Solution". But in order to succeed, you have to first understand what sort of business model is correct for you and the pros and cons of each.

In this chapter, I'm going to analyze the top three business models available online in order to help you derive the essential knowledge to make the most profitable conclusion for you and your future.

What's Right For You

Selection 1: Market a "Biz Opp" or System

There are a lot of different companies out there who give you the chance to recruit others into the same business arrangement. This is what I refer to as a "Biz Op." There are numerous main sorts of a Business Opportunity.

A. Multi-Level Marketing

This concept is decidedly not new and chances are, you're familiar with it. MLM has obtained a mediocre reputation amid some groups, as many individuals believe it's associated with a Ponzi scheme. But, this bad report is a result of individuals trying to sell it as something that it's not.

That coupled with the fact that most individuals simply don't know how to sell, which is an essential for most MLM companies—it's incurred a bad reputation. But, MLM is really a pretty good business model if you view the facts.

In most MLM companies, you get paid in 2 basic ways:

1. You get paid a commission upon product sales. You are paid a commission if you recruit somebody into the business, by way of their product sales, or maybe a commission paid on their "start Kit".

2. You likewise are paid a residual revenue based upon the sales of your downline (individuals who are signed on underneath you). Commonly, an MLM company collects all product payments and then

you get a commission on a weekly or bi-weekly basis. One facet of the MLM Business Model that may be extremely good is the residual income. Contrary to other business models, in MLM you've the Chance to create a residual revenue—which means even when you're not bringing in sales yourself, you're still being paid on the sales of your downline.

Traditionally, MLM requires more time to build during the first couple of years, but then you may start to experience a residual income that may far exceed your own sales commissions. This means, over time, you've the chance to work less while still getting paid.

B. Direct Sales

Direct Sales has grown in fame over the last 4-5 years, particularly in the "Make Money Online" industry. Direct Sales merely means that you get paid a direct commission from sales that you attain.

In most Direct Sales companies, you get paid in the accompanying ways:

1. Commission on Product Sales

Commission is brought in when you sign somebody up in the business opportunity, the commission commonly coming from their product buy.

In a few Direct Sales companies, you might be the one collecting the funds for product sales. You then hold your commission up front and send in the wholesale amount to the company. Clearly, this is one advantage of some Direct Sales companies—you are paid at once.

A few Direct Sales companies do provide a residual income as well as the up-front commissions. But most of your revenue will come from the commissions on sales that you personally bring in. One major advantage of marketing a Direct Sales-type business opportunity is that you may bring in significantly higher profits and faster than you may with an MLM company. On the flipside, you don't have the long-run advantage of a substantial residual revenue.

C. Marketing a Marketing System

This choice is one that many individuals, whether they're in an MLM or Direct Sales business, sell on the front-end.

Here's how it goes:

- You drive hits to XYZ Marketing System site.
- You get somebody signed on in the Marketing System.
- Once they're signed on, you (or your sites) present them with your business opportunity.

While this selection may work, it can likewise become exceedingly convoluted and confusing for the prospect. After all, what you're basically doing is selling somebody on XYZ Marketing System first of all, and then selling your business concern—rather than simply selling him/her on the business concern directly.

Option 2: Sell another persons Product

Now you may be thinking, "How is this unlike Option #1? Aren't I selling others products in #1?" The answer to that is uh-huh. In Option #1, marketing a Business Opportunity / System— you're

selling another persons products. But what I'm mentioning specifically here in Option #2 is the selling of the actual merchandise directly, and not the Business Opportunity or the System.

For instance, in order to be successful at marketing a business opportunity, most of the success and earnings develop as a result of promoting the actual opportunity, or the "story". The real product itself isn't commonly the main headlining feature on the front-end. Naturally, the products would be mentioned on the back-end, but most individuals lead with the opportunity and not the products.

What we're bringing up here is straight product sales. There are many primary types of platforms to sell other peoples' products.

Affiliate Marketing

Affiliate Marketing is the perfect instance of selling another person's products. Here a few examples of sorts of products you may sell as an affiliate marketer:

- E-books
- Web Based Software / Tools
- Educational Products
- Training

The most perceptible advantage of selling another persons product is that you don't have to produce the product. Most companies that provide affiliate programs likewise provide you with the marketing materials you require to sell the product.

As I mentioned, you don't have to in reality produce the product yourself. Additionally, the majority of individuals who allow others to earn a commission on selling their products already have sites and marketing materials ready for you.

Option 3: produce and Sell Your Own Product

This choice refers to you really making your very own unique product from scratch and selling it in the market.

For instance, if you had a unique marketing technique, you may produce your own info product and sell it. You may likewise allow others to sell it through an affiliate program.

While this is thought to be the height of Net Marketing success—having your own products—this isn't for the majority of individuals online.

That's not to state that it can't be accomplished—individuals do it all the time. But to accomplish it successfully, it really takes a lot:

You should now have a deeper understanding of how the "Make Money Online" industry functions and what the different options are to have your own Net Business.

Chapter 5:
Being A Success On The Net

Synopsis

Over the years, I was involved in countless Net business ventures. Some didn't work and some were highly successful. After a lot of years of being involved with the Net and learning how to create, package and bring a product to market—I learned a couple of things:

- Technology shifts quickly, but human nature doesn't.
- Producing a product from scratch has tremendous advantages, but there are many other ways to generate a profit online (
- Offering individuals packaged solutions frequently results in greater profits.
- The technology we utilize to do business might constantly shift, but sound business and marketing practices don't.
- Having a panoramic view of many different industries will always bring you greater success.
- Perpetually challenging your own view and the status quo will bring you the highest rewards.

With this knowledge and experience beneath my belt, I recognized that I wanted to continue leveraging the Net. But, I was no longer interested in working "hard". I chose to leverage "O.P.P." - Other People's Products.

About Products

Producing a product and/or business from the ground up may be stimulating. But it's not precisely a walk in the park. I needed to find that balance of continuing to bring forth profits from the Net while still having the time to LIVE!

When I first made the decision that I wished to sell a ready-made products online, I did what many individuals do and joined a System that gave a whole "package deal". The sites were already created for you. There was training, a community of individuals, and products that were ready to sell with a great compensation plan. It got fairly obvious after signing on that what was initially advertised on the front-end didn't match the truth of the back-end.

What I mean is: what was being distributed on the front-end, "a plug-and-play system, no calls, etc. etc". Didn't match up with the truth of what it would actually call for to yield a profit.

Rather than carrying on to be a number amongst the masses, I chose to head out on my own and discover a real mentor. Not a "sponsor" or somebody that I simply listened to on training calls, but somebody who had been in that particular industry for a while. Somebody that "knew the ropes" and could help me craft my game plan for success.

After I chose to go out on my own with the guidance of my mentor, I recognized that branding myself was exceedingly crucial. But none in the sense that most individuals think of: adding a picture and story to a generic site template. I chose to produce a brand that not only represented my values and notions, but delivered an unparalleled offering that the market was hungry for: The reality about how this industry functions.

In doing so, I recognized I may ruffle a couple of feathers here and there, but that was a little price to pay for the gratification of knowing I could stand 100% behind what I was marketing.
The bottom line: I knew I would not be able to produce a sustainable business by selling something that plainly wasn't true.

I wasn't okay with selling "hope in a site". But what I did wish to do is sell something tangible—that didn't have any hidden aspects to it, that individuals could comprehend up front. As a consequence of doing so, that shift in my business was like night and day. It was no more about attempting to hide behind a fabricated facade. It was about marketing myself, the products I represented, and what I trusted in.

When you trust 100% in what you're marketing, making revenue becomes so much easier. You're able to have aboveboard conversations with individuals rather than attempting to push them into an "automated" and twisted system of different levels.

Basically what I've done is leveraged another persons product, but with my brand on the front. But what's crucial: I decided to get rid of the marketing system, which means doing away with the confusing steps that only water down conversions.

So rather than sending individuals through a multi-step, I erased all the middle steps, so it works like this:

Generate Lead > Convert to Sale

This is much more direct than what most marketing schemes will provide you with. It likewise demands that you're comfortable going out on your own. You'll likewise have to acquire new skill sets. It's like anything else. If you wish to become a physician, you have to go to medical school before you make the big money.

If you wish to have a successful Net business, you have to learn about numbers, conversions, copywriting, branding, social media and lead propagation. There's no way around that, in spite of what all the hoopla online says.

Arranging your business in a way that's 100% unequalled to you while selling a readymade product on the back-end has the following advantages:

- Have complete command over your marketing content.
- Decide what sort of individuals you want to work with.
- Feel 100% proud of your business.
- Establish your own brand rather than another persons.
- The power to have total command over your sites.
- Having the freedom to be on your own rather than being at the mercy of what the owners of the marketing system feel like doing to better their own profits (not yours).
- Market a product that's already made and proven to sell, without having to make it yourself.
- Spend less on advertisement and bring in a lot of sales.

Here's the primary point I truly wish you to consider: What is the primary goal of your business? The primary goal of your business is to bring in sales so you may generate a profit, correct? Correct.

So wouldn't it add up then, to discover the quickest route from Lead to Sale, with minimum overhead? Utterly!

Recognize that each time you add a step into your marketing funnel; you're diminishing conversions from lead to sale. What I'm advocating, is to... Cut off the "middleman".

In this case, the middleman is the purportedly automated multi-step Marketing System. Consider it: All the system is doing is placing a lot of unneeded steps in between a site visitor and a high commission sale being made. And the cost of having all these unneeded steps is a cost to YOU. Revenue is made on the part of the middleman (the System owners), but you're paying for this profit out of your own pocket with your membership fees, front-end products and ad dollars spent.

Illustration: you've a hundred leads...

Lead > $49 Front-end > $500 Upsell > $2000 Upsell > $8000 Upsell > $12000 Upsell

If each step of the marketing funnel converts at 10% (which is really high), that means:

- Leads = 100
- $49 Front-end = 10
- $500 Upsell = 1

That means you drained leads at the second step of the process. This means if you were able to yield leads at a cost of $5 a lead, the 100 leads cost you $500. So you spent $500 on the leads and you made a

commission of $20 on the front-end sale. And a $400 commission on the $500 upsell, you made $420. So you really lost $80 and no one made it to the $2000 upsell point.

This is precisely what occurs with most individuals who join a plan that has many steps involved in their sales procedure. The members don't have a truthful viewpoint of the bottom-line numbers, and how would they? The only info about conversions is what the plan owner's state. If more members really did their own math—rather than going by what others state—many individuals would be making really different business choices.

The biggest issue is that everybody seems to forget the primary purpose of the business, which is to make revenue. Rather, individuals get distracted with selling front-end applications, kits and low-level products. Few ever make it past that point to really yield a profit on a uniform basis.

Generating leads isn't the goal. Yielding an income is. Big difference. Most individuals are going for the leads, and that's it.

There are a lot of one-hit-wonders online, which represent most of the "success stories" and "recommendations" that you see on sites.

But again, the goal of a business ought to be to yield an income on a uniform basis.

Chapter 6:
What You Need To Profit

Synopsis

Below is an outline of the precise tools and resources you'll require to produce a business that's establishing YOUR brand and YOUR earnings.

Take A Good Look

1. Mentor

Here are the standards that ought to be utilized when picking out a mentor:
- Does this individual have a record of success?
- Does this individual have a vested financial concern in your success?
- Do you like this individual?
- Does this individual share your center beliefs and values?
- What specifically will you be able to learn from this individual?
- What experience does this individual have—outside of the industry—that may be beneficial to your own success?
- Does this individual have a true interest in helping you succeed, or are there additional motives involved?

There are a lot of different places to find a mentor. The more you start networking within the industry and speaking with individuals, the more likely you are to be able to meet somebody who may become your mentor.

2. Brand

There's a lot of babble about "Personal Branding" these days. In a nutshell, a brand isn't necessarily what is stated on a site. A brand is what your leads think of when they hear your name. There are a lot of branding "elements" which serve the purpose of bringing the intangible brand into a tangible form.

These factors include the name, logo, color scheme, tagline or any additional particular visual or text elements that try to define a brand. But once again, a brand has been accomplished when a name / product name / company name is said, and this arouses feelings,

images, and reference points in the audience's mind. Your brand is basically the sum of all characteristics that make you unique. It's the total of all these things, not simply one. Trust is likewise a main component of successful branding.

Many individuals have a difficult time coming up with their own brand. Here's the best way to get going:
- Consider someone you know who's nothing like you.
- Make a list of everything that's unique about you, as compared to this other individual. This ought to include everything from background and experiences to likes, wants and opinions.

This ought to get the wheels turning in your head about why you're unique. It's not the comparison in #2 that matters, but it's an excellent way to start realizing that you've many unique points about you. As they say, there's only one YOU!

Here are some fast tips in relation to your brand and what will fetch attention:
- Consider what your audience wants.
- What issues do they presently face?
- Which one of YOUR unique features could help solve their issues?

Those are the features you wish to highlight in your branding, those which are relevant to solving the issues of your audience.

3. Web site

On the Net, your site is a huge component of your net identity. It's not the sole thing, but it's definitely a major part of it. When doing business online, your personal site is precisely like an initial face-to face meeting with somebody. Your site is your online "first

impression". Individuals will respect you, only to the degree that you respect yourself. Take pride in yourself, in what you're providing.

There are a lot of different choices online to produce a site. It's better to save up and hire someone if you have to and get something that looks dynamite instead of trying to do something yourself that's going to look homemade. Get the best! You merit it, your image deserves it, and so does your business!

4. Landing Page(s)

A "Landing Page" has only a single purpose: to convert a visitor into a lead. That's it. The aim of a landing page isn't to sell your story, your products, your system or anything additional. The aim of a landing page is to sell the "opt-in" and get the individual on your list.

You purposely take-charge of what a lead does and where they go on a landing page.

You want them to opt-in, so you don't give them any other options than to opt in or leave the site. Your list is among the most valuable assets you have in a Net business. But the reality is, the goal isn't simply to build a list of good size, but a list that's quality—with which you may build a long-term relationship.

Here are the primary elements of a successful landing page:

A. The "how come"

Before you dive into producing a landing page, or having somebody produce one for you, you have to be clear on what the offer of the landing page IS. The offer ought to answer the question, "Why is somebody going to desire to fill out the form on the landing page?"

Here's a list of typically utilized offers:

- Gratis report
- Gratis video
- Gratis e-zine
- Gratis Trial Offer
- Info about how somebody accomplished something
- Info about how a issue was solved

The main point is to consider what issues your prospect has. How you may get the process started of providing a solution to that issue through the offer on your landing page?

B. Headline

The headline is the most crucial thing on the page. That's why a lot of times you see headlines in red, to get the reader's attention.
If the headline is great, then you've a better chance of keeping the visitor on the page. And, as a result, you've a better chance of converting that visitor into a lead.

Many of the most successful headlines express the advantages of an offer through a story that's told in very few words. Learning how to author great headlines takes experience, testing and copywriting skills. These are not things that are learned overnight. But if you understand how to type an email message, chances are—you can learn a few basic copywriting techniques.

C. Really Short Copy

Here's where individuals get distracted with landing pages. The natural want is to put too much info on the landing page. The tendency with landing pages is to attempt and sell the whole "kit and kaboodle" when all you truly need to sell is the "opt-in"—to get the individual to fill out the form. Consider it this way: If you tell

everybody everything there is to know about you and your products on the landing page, what grounds do they have to give you their valuable contact info? I advocate having about 100 words or less of short copy on the landing page— perhaps a bulleted list of 4-5 quick points, and that's it.

D. Opt-in Form

Now that you've your visitor's attention, you above all wish to capture their e-mail address. In order to be able to capture a visitor's info, you require an "opt-in form". This is precisely what it sounds like. The form on a site that a visitor would fill out with their e-mail address (and possibly other information).

A crucial thing to realize about opt-in forms is that each field you add (Name, Email, Phone, Address) diminishes conversion, but increases quality. So you have to take into consideration what info is utterly necessary for you to collect on your landing page and adapt accordingly.

In order to have the form appear on the site, you require a third-party software. The most popular ones include Aweber, iContact, Constant Contact, or InfusionSoft. Once you've signed on for the third-party software, you (or your web designer) will produce the form, and get the HTML code. This code is then embedded into your landing page. Now when individuals fill out the form on your site, their contact info is stored within your database.

e. Product

As I adverted earlier, when I decided to sell a product that was ready to go. Not only did this save me the time and resources from having to produce a product from scratch, but I could select something that already had an firm track record of selling, decreasing the risk.

How to assess the product...

Q. Is The Product Sold By Itself?
Is this product affiliated to a business opportunity? If yes, do individuals truly purchase the product outside of that? Pick a product that individuals would actually purchase—just for the product itself.

Q. Do You Believe In It 100%?
You wish to pick a product that YOU believe in. As I mentioned earlier, when you trust in something, it's a heck of a lot simpler to make revenue selling it. You're excited about it, excited to promote it, and are surefooted in discussing it with your prospects.

Q. Is The Product Relevant?
Following, you need to make certain that the product is relevant to what is occurring today, and what will be happening in the really near future. Does this product solve a major issue for individuals in today's world?"

f. Sales Process
Now that you've a Product, Site and Landing Page, you require a solid sales process to help you yield the profits. Whatever you're doing in life, you're a sales person. Whether you like to utilize the term "selling" or not, that's what we do in life.

We sell individuals on being our friends, on being our mate, on being our business partner, and purchasing from us. We may likewise sell individuals on not doing business with us, not being our friends, or not seeing our viewpoint.

Whether you're selling some a positive or negative end result, you're selling either way.

The truth of the matter is: if you wish to make a killing online—or in any business for that matter—you have to learn not only how to face rejection, but alter your position of what rejection truly is. Most of the time, rejection happens when a prospect doesn't trust you or feels that inaction is a choice.

Your greatest obstacle isn't in getting individuals to choose you over the competition, but it's in getting them to choose you versus doing nothing. The main way to defeat the obstacle of individuals doing nothing is through effective personal communication.

Whether it's accomplished by copywriting or a phone conversation, overcome objections is your #1 obstacle to yielding profits.

The truth is, if you abide by my advice when selecting a product and sell something you believe in 100%, you don't have to have "sales skills" to make sales. You merely need to trust in what you're selling, and that rubs off on your prospects immediately.

Chapter 7:
Integrity

Synopsis

Integrity is taking action in a manner that's in line with your declared values. Many individuals confuse integrity with morals and ethics. According to Wikipedia, "Integrity is a concept of consistency of actions, values, techniques, measures, principles, expectation and results."

Chapter 7:
Integrity

Synopsis

Integrity is taking action in a manner that's in line with your declared values. Many individuals confuse integrity with morals and ethics. According to Wikipedia, "Integrity is a concept of consistency of actions, values, techniques, measures, principles, expectation and results."

individuals on not doing business with us, not being our friends, or not seeing our viewpoint.

Whether you're selling some a positive or negative end result, you're selling either way.

The truth of the matter is: if you wish to make a killing online—or in any business for that matter—you have to learn not only how to face rejection, but alter your position of what rejection truly is. Most of the time, rejection happens when a prospect doesn't trust you or feels that inaction is a choice.

Your greatest obstacle isn't in getting individuals to choose you over the competition, but it's in getting them to choose you versus doing nothing. The main way to defeat the obstacle of individuals doing nothing is through effective personal communication.

Whether it's accomplished by copywriting or a phone conversation, overcome objections is your #1 obstacle to yielding profits.

The truth is, if you abide by my advice when selecting a product and sell something you believe in 100%, you don't have to have "sales skills" to make sales. You merely need to trust in what you're selling, and that rubs off on your prospects immediately.

Look At Yourself

To act with integrity means that your actions match your stated beliefs and values.

To act out of integrity means your actions don't match up with your stated values and beliefs. For instance, if a marketer states on his site, "I value helping other people succeed", but then he doesn't take action to help other people succeed—he's out of integrity.

But, if a marketer states on his site, "I value helping myself succeed", and he takes action to help himself succeed—then he has integrity. Integrity isn't about being correct or incorrect. It's about actions matching up with stating values and beliefs.

The most significant thing, particularly if you're an individual marketing yourself online, is that you have integrity with yourself. If you don't have that, you may never have it with anybody else. What are your opinions? What do you time value? What is significant to you?

Does what you offer, and how you depict your business, have integrity? Do the actions you take online match up with your core beliefs?

That is step #1 in success. If your actions don't match-up with your core values and beliefs—if integrity doesn't exist—attempting to accomplish success will be an uphill battle.

But, when what you provide is in line with your core values and beliefs, any resistance appears to dissipate without notice.

It's not a "fight" of getting individuals to purchase stuff. It's merely a matter of sharing what is already there. The whole process of making revenue becomes fun and enjoyable.

Let's face it: we don't have a limitless number of days on this earth. There's no point in "struggling" to make revenue when you may have fun making money. This is the advantage of building a legacy with integrity.

Producing a successful business, regardless if it's online or a traditional business, takes a lot of "blood, sweat and tears".

The last thing you wish is to put in all of this work, and have nothing to show for it.

Wrapping Up

"Knowledge Is Power." The more you understand about what you're involved with, the better decisions you're able to arrive at. Clearly, it's inconceivable to know everything about any given area. In life, there are forever inherent risks. But the more knowledge you have about an area, the less speculative it becomes.

In order to preserve your legacy, there's a particular level of knowledge that you have to acquire. Just like Robert Kiyosaki says, "Becoming wealthy isn't about how much money you make, it's about how much money you keep."

- I want to make certain you truly comprehend that good financial habits have to begin now, wherever you are. The last thing you want to do, is be making $100K a month, but still be broke.
- Start making a habit of reserving money weekly. The amount if not crucial, it could even be only $5. Make a commitment that you're going to preserve the legacy you're working so hard to build.
- In order to produce good financial management habits, you have to know what's coming and what's going out.
- Bear in mind, if you're going to operate a business in the Net marketing world, it's a business.
- Use a mentor.
- Keep your eyes and ears open. It's amazing what opportunities present themselves if you're brain is actively seeking an answer. Talk to people, ask for advice and see if somebody in your personal network has any recommendations.

I hope you found this e-Book valuable, and above all, I hope it challenged you to question "authority" and make your own path.

www.ingramcontent.com/pod-product-compliance
Lightning Source LLC
Chambersburg PA
CBHW030527220526
45463CB00007B/2751